PSALM REFRAINS

Reproducible Calligraphic Expressions of Sunday Responsorials

Foreword by Mary Jo Tully
Chancellor, Archdiocese of Portland, Oregon

Calligraphic clip art by Charles Lehman

Sheed & Ward
Kansas City

THE SCRIBE

Charles Lehman lives with his wife Erma and son David in Portland, OR. He was trained in the craft of calligraphy by Lloyd Reynolds and Arnold Bank. Lehman now teaches and produces calligraphy for exhibition and commercial assignments.

Sheed & Ward™ is a service of The National Catholic Reporter Publishing Company.

ISBN: 1-55612-855-X

Published by: Sheed & Ward
                 115 E. Armour Blvd.
                 P.O. Box 419492
                 Kansas City, MO 64141-6492

To order, call: (800) 333-7373

DEDICATION

This book is dedicated with my deep love to my
grandchildren

Joel, Jamie, Katie & Paul.

FOREWORD

It was the coldest day in the history of our city. The skies were gray, the streets icy. Finally, the ceremonies were over. I could scarcely remember them because my grief was so fresh. There is little doubt that the Church had done what it always does. It had gathered to take the place where my Dad had once stood, but – as always – there was still a large void. For a time, I was consoled by the presence of so many people who cared about my Dad, about my family.

In the back of my mind, the words of the Psalm Refrain echoed: "The Lord is my Shepherd, I shall not want." The melody and the words ran through my thoughts like a theme. In retrospect, I know that this is, indeed, what the Psalm Refrains ought to do.

While my example might well be the most dramatic that could be chosen, it makes a point that has a pastoral implication for those who plan liturgical celebrations. We ought to pay more attention to the Psalms for they carry the weight of poetry and have the power to evoke the religious emotions that set off the religious signals that change our lives. They can be the avenues we walk that underline the sacredness of everything that surrounds us.

Despite the fact that increasing numbers of Catholics are reading and studying the Scripture, it will likely take another generation before the average Catholic is comfortable with the Bible, particularly the Hebrew Scripture. The Psalms, simply because they are easily seen as poetry and open to emotive interpretation, are one of the most accessible paths for those who would see Scripture as integral to the Christian life.

The history of revelation seems deceptively simple. Briefly, the Father spoke. His people did not hear. He spoke again and again and again. One need only read the Old Testament as an account of the Father revealing himself again and again to discover a persistent God intent on showing himself to his people.

And then, God sent the Word, Jesus, who would enflesh his word. Today, Jesus – through the teaching authority of the Church – is the Guarantor of God's Word. In Jesus, the message of the Old Law was fulfilled, the fullness of God's message communicated. At the time of the apostles, the message was completed.

Despite this deceptive simplicity, there is much to be said about revelation as Catholics understand it. God reveals himself, first of all, by acting in people's real lives. God is so much a part of our lives that we encounter him in our day to day living. He has gifted us with an intelligence and, even more, with faith so that we might discover him again and again in our midst. Faith gives God's intelligent creatures insight and sensitivity to what is taking place. Sometimes God's activity is so apparent that we who have faith can scarcely avoid discovering him. Who, after all, can ignore the power and majesty of a God who can create the heavens, the mountains, the oceans? Who can look at a newborn baby without faith? And, faith is the believer's surrender to God's revelation of himself.

Secondly, God reveals himself by preparing us for insight into his activity. This revelation is not just an explanation of the God we know; it is a presentation of God acting in history as savior, a redeeming God who saves people from slavery and brings them to freedom. This awareness of God's action as saving is a special penetration into God's activity provided by God who gave certain persons within the nation he chose the help they needed to come to this special insight call **inspiration**.

Scripture, then, is not so much an account of God's mighty acts alone, but also – and this is really more important – an act of revelation. Catholics believe that the Bible is normative revelation given to them so that through it they may become aware of the saving activity of God in their lives. The reader sees God in the past so that his vision may be properly prepared to see him in the present.

Christians, and before us the Jews, are the recipients of a unique understanding of God. Throughout the ages, other religious traditions have provided an explanation of the creative acts of the gods. They told tales of the gods, described how it was that the gods lived and where they lived. But in all instances, the gods lived in a mythical place and in a mythical time. But, with Israel, a religious revolution took place. The revolution consisted in a new theophany: the intervention of God in history. This is an understanding derived from creation – an assertion that God chose to make certain events his own – heightened occasions of revelation. Just as in marriage there are heightened expressions of fidelity to a partner along side a life which is itself a revelation of that fidelity.

Each such theophany is irreversible and unrepeatable. The fall of Jerusalem does not repeat the fall of Samaria. The ruin of Jerusalem presents a new historic theophany. Such deeds reveal the power attached to a person, Yahweh – not a transpersonal power. Because he is a Person, a Being enjoying perfect freedom, Yahweh stands out from the world of abstractions, symbols and generalities. He acts in history and enters into relationship with historical beings. And when God "shows" himself in a radical and complete manner by becoming incarnate in Jesus Christ, then *all* history becomes a theophany.

In Judaism, then, and above all in Christianity, divinity manifested itself in history. Christ and his contemporaries were part of history. The Son of God, by his incarnation, accepted existence in history.

Revelation is what occurs in the flesh of each historical being. But every occurrence need not be interpreted as revelation by the person. A believer cannot repudiate history, but neither can he accept it all. He must continually choose, in the tangle of historical events, that which is charged with saving significance.

Because the Scripture is the story of human experience in God, those who have a greater wealth of experience and awareness are better able to enter into the faith dimension of these living words. Adults are able to look for echoes in their own experience. The Psalms enable us to exclaim rather than explain. We are able, in other words, to pray the Scripture. At liturgy, we gather to "stand under" the Word of God rather than to merely understand it.

The Psalms speak powerfully because they are poetry. But understanding their poetic structure is less important than letting them speak to our hearts. A famous poet once said, "A poem should not mean, but be!" This is the attitude with which we ought to approach the Psalms at liturgy. Help those who worship to hear with their hearts. Choose music that will help the refrain echo throughout the day, throughout the week. Choose art that will pick up the refrain and unite the readings. The calligraphy is presented in this spirit.

In short, let the Psalms speak of what the people know and believe. We have a loving relationship to the Father and to one another through Jesus. It's enough to make us want to sing.

Mary Jo Tully

INTRODUCTION

SUGGESTIONS FOR THE USE OF THIS BOOK

T his book provides calligraphic renditions of the Psalm Refrains from the Propers of the Mass throughout the liturgical year. A variety of historically sound forms of calligraphy – seven different hands, representing the finest and most important models that span the history of western culture – have been used to write the sacred texts with the traditional broad-edged pen. The dance of the pen and rhythmic patterns of the writing offer a kind of music for the eyes of the readers. As the eye "listens," the visual beauty attracts the reader to embrace the psalm as something worthwhile in itself as a personal prayer.

The calligraphy is intended primarily as clip art to enhance parish publications of all sorts. For this reason the pages are printed in black ink on one side only to make it easier to use the book on a copy machine or scanner. Typically a parish bulletin is printed on 8 1/2" x 11" paper, either as a single sheet or on 11" x 17" paper folded once to the same size. The page size is approximately 3:4 (w:h) in proportion. The calligraphic presentations of the Psalm Refrains in this book range in length suitable for use as headlines on this page size. The calligraphy will look best as a headline centered on the page above text blocks with generous margins: top 1", left and right side 1 1/2", base 2".

 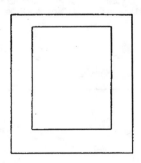 

After a calligraphy headline is added to a page, leave breathing space above and below when adding text. If the calligraphy is simply a space filler unrelated to typed copy, a solid line above and below effectively divides the calligraphy from text. If the margins suggested above are used, the entire composition, calligraphy and typed text, will fill a rectangle equal to about half of the space of the page and it will be in proportion to the page itself – a good design. Once the layout of the page is designed, use a copy machine to create black and white copies from this book of whatever Psalm Refrain is desired for the publication. Enlarge or reduce the size of the calligraphy at will for different effects or layouts.

Despite this deceptive simplicity, there is much to be said about revelation as Catholics understand it. God reveals himself, first of all, by acting in people's real lives. God is so much a part of our lives that we encounter him in our day to day living. He has gifted us with an intelligence and, even more, with faith so that we might discover him again and again in our midst. Faith gives God's intelligent creatures insight and sensitivity to what is taking place. Sometimes God's activity is so apparent that we who have faith can scarcely avoid discovering him. Who, after all, can ignore the power and majesty of a God who can create the heavens, the mountains, the oceans? Who can look at a newborn baby without faith? And, faith is the believer's surrender to God's revelation of himself.

A light will shine on us this day: the Lord is born for us.

Scripture, then, is not so much an account of God's mighty acts alone, but also--and this is really more important--an act of revelation. Catholics believe that the Bible is normative revelation given to them so that through it they may become aware of the saving activity of God in their lives. The reader sees God in the past so that his vision may be properly prepared to see him in the present.

Christians, and before us the Jews, are the recipients of a unique understanding of God. Throughout the ages, other religious traditions have provided an explanation of the creative acts of the gods. They

I rejoiced when I heard them say: let us go to the house of the Lord.

PSALM REFRAIN - FIRST SUNDAY OF ADVENT - CYCLE A

Lord, make us turn to you, let us see your face and we shall be saved.

PSALM REFRAIN - FIRST SUNDAY OF ADVENT - CYCLE B

TO YOU, O LORD, I LIFT MY SOUL.

PSALM REFRAIN - FIRST SUNDAY OF ADVENT - CYCLE C

JUSTICE SHALL FLOURISH IN HIS TIME, AND FULLNESS OF PEACE FOR EVER.

PSALM REFRAIN - SECOND SUNDAY OF ADVENT - CYCLE A

Lord, let us see your kindness and grant us your salvation.

PSALM REFRAIN - SECOND SUNDAY OF ADVENT - CYCLE B

The Lord has done great things for us; we are filled with joy.

PSALM REFRAIN - SECOND SUNDAY OF ADVENT - CYCLE C

LORD, COME AND SAVE US.

PSALM REFRAIN - THIRD SUNDAY OF ADVENT - CYCLE A

My soul rejoices in my God.

PSALM REFRAIN - THIRD SUNDAY OF ADVENT - CYCLE B

Cry out with joy and gladness: for among you is the great and holy One of Israel.

PSALM REFRAIN - THIRD SUNDAY OF ADVENT - CYCLE C

LET THE LORD ENTER; HE IS KING OF GLORY.

PSALM REFRAIN - FOURTH SUNDAY OF ADVENT - CYCLE A

FOR EVER I WILL SING THE GOODNESS OF THE LORD.

PSALM REFRAIN - FOURTH SUNDAY OF ADVENT - CYCLE B

Lord, make us turn to you, let us see your face and we shall be saved.

PSALM REFRAIN - FOURTH SUNDAY OF ADVENT - CYCLE C

FOR EVER I WILL SING THE GOODNESS OF THE LORD.

PSALM REFRAIN - CHRISTMAS VIGIL - CYCLES ABC

Today is born our savior, Christ the Lord.

PSALM REFRAIN - CHRISTMAS MASS AT MIDNIGHT - CYCLES ABC

A light will shine on us this day: the Lord is born for us.

PSALM REFRAIN - CHRISTMAS MASS AT DAWN - CYCLES ABC

All the ends of the earth have seen the saving power of God.

PSALM REFRAIN - CHRISTMAS MASS DURING THE DAY - CYCLES ABC

Happy are those who fear the Lord and walk in his ways.

PSALM REFRAIN - SUNDAY IN THE OCTAVE OF CHRISTMAS
HOLY FAMILY - CYCLES ABC

MAY GOD BLESS US IN HIS MERCY.

PSALM REFRAIN - JANUARY 1 - OCTAVE OF CHRISTMAS
SOLEMNITY OF MARY, MOTHER OF GOD - CYCLES ABC

The Word of God became man, and lived among us.

PSALM REFRAIN - SECOND SUNDAY AFTER CHRISTMAS - CYCLES ABC

LORD, EVERY NATION ON EARTH WILL ADORE YOU.

PSALM REFRAIN - JANUARY 6 - EPIPHANY - CYCLES ABC

THE LORD WILL BLESS HIS PEOPLE WITH PEACE.

PSALM REFRAIN - SUNDAY AFTER JANUARY 6 - BAPTISM OF THE LORD - CYCLES ABC

BE MERCIFUL, O LORD, FOR WE HAVE SINNED.

PSALM REFRAIN - FIRST SUNDAY OF LENT - CYCLE A

Your ways, O Lord, are love and truth, to those who keep your covenant.

PSALM REFRAIN - FIRST SUNDAY OF LENT - CYCLE B

Be with me Lord, when I am in trouble.

PSALM REFRAIN - FIRST SUNDAY OF LENT - CYCLE C

Lord, let your mercy be on us, as we place our trust in you.

PSALM REFRAIN - SECOND SUNDAY OF LENT - CYCLE A

I will walk in the presence of the Lord, in the land of the living.

PSALM REFRAIN - SECOND SUNDAY OF LENT - CYCLE B

THE LORD IS MY LIGHT AND MY SALVATION.

PSALM REFRAIN - SECOND SUNDAY OF LENT - CYCLE C

IF TODAY YOU HEAR HIS VOICE, HARDEN NOT YOUR HEARTS.

PSALM REFRAIN - THIRD SUNDAY OF LENT - CYCLE A

LORD, YOU HAVE THE WORDS OF EVERLASTING LIFE.

PSALM REFRAIN - THIRD SUNDAY OF LENT - CYCLE B

The Lord is kind and merciful.

PSALM REFRAIN - THIRD SUNDAY OF LENT - CYCLE C

The Lord is my shepherd, there is nothing I shall want.

PSALM REFRAIN - FOURTH SUNDAY OF LENT - CYCLE A

Let my tongue be silenced, if I ever forget you!

PSALM REFRAIN - FOURTH SUNDAY OF LENT - CYCLE B

Taste and see the goodness of the Lord.

PSALM REFRAIN - FOURTH SUNDAY OF LENT - CYCLE C

WITH THE LORD THERE IS MERCY, AND FULLNESS OF REDEMPTION.

PSALM REFRAIN - FIFTH SUNDAY OF LENT - CYCLE A

CREATE A CLEAN HEART IN ME, O GOD.

PSALM REFRAIN - FIFTH SUNDAY OF LENT - CYCLE B

THE LORD HAS DONE GREAT THINGS FOR US; WE ARE FILLED WITH JOY.

PSALM REFRAIN - FIFTH SUNDAY OF LENT - CYCLE C

My God, my God, why have you abandoned me?

PSALM REFRAIN - PASSION SUNDAY (PALM SUNDAY) - CYCLES ABC

ffor ever I will sing the goodness of the Lord.

PSALM REFRAIN - HOLY THURSDAY - CHRISM MASS - CYCLES ABC

Our blessing-cup is a communion with the blood of Christ.

PSALM REFRAIN - HOLY THURSDAY - MASS OF THE LORD'S SUPPER - CYCLES ABC

Father, I put my life in your hands.

PSALM REFRAIN - GOOD FRIDAY - CYCLES ABC

LORD, SEND OUT YOUR SPIRIT, AND RENEW THE FACE OF THE EARTH.

PSALM REFRAIN - EASTER VIGIL (AFTER READING 1) - CYCLES ABC

THE EARTH IS FULL OF THE GOODNESS OF THE LORD.

PSALM REFRAIN - EASTER VIGIL (ALTERNATE AFTER READING 1) - CYCLES ABC

KEEP ME SAFE, O GOD; YOU ARE MY HOPE.

PSALM REFRAIN - EASTER VIGIL (AFTER READING 2) - CYCLES ABC

Let us sing to the Lord, he has covered himself in glory

PSALM REFRAIN - EASTER VIGIL (AFTER READING 3) - CYCLES ABC

I will praise you, Lord, for you have rescued me.

PSALM REFRAIN - EASTER VIGIL (AFTER READING 4) - CYCLES ABC

You will draw water joyfully from the springs of salvation.

PSALM REFRAIN - EASTER VIGIL (AFTER READING 5) - CYCLES ABC

LORD, YOU HAVE THE WORDS OF EVERLASTING LIFE

PSALM REFRAIN - EASTER VIGIL (AFTER READING 6) - CYCLES ABC

Like a deer that longs for running streams, my soul longs for you, my God.

PSALM REFRAIN - EASTER VIGIL (AFTER READING 7) - CYCLES ABC

CREATE A CLEAN HEART IN ME, O GOD.

PSALM REFRAIN - EASTER VIGIL (ALTERNATE AFTER READING 7) - CYCLES ABC

ALLELUIA. ALLELUIA. ALLELUIA.

PSALM REFRAIN - EASTER VIGIL (AFTER THE EPISTLE) - CYCLES ABC

This is the day the Lord has made, let us rejoice and be glad.

PSALM REFRAIN - EASTER SUNDAY - CYCLES ABC

Give thanks to the Lord for he is good, his love is everlasting.

PSALM REFRAIN - SECOND SUNDAY OF EASTER - CYCLE S ABC

Lord, you will show us the path of life.

PSALM REFRAIN - THIRD SUNDAY OF EASTER - CYCLE A

Lord, let your face shine on us.

PSALM REFRAIN - THIRD SUNDAY OF EASTER - CYCLE B

I will praise you, Lord, for you have rescued me.

PSALM REFRAIN - THIRD SUNDAY OF EASTER - CYCLE C

THE LORD IS MY SHEPHERD, THERE IS NOTHING I SHALL WANT.

PSALM REFRAIN - FOURTH SUNDAY OF EASTER - CYCLE A

THE STONE REJECTED BY THE BUILDERS HAS BECOME THE CORNERSTONE.

PSALM REFRAIN - FOURTH SUNDAY OF EASTER - CYCLE B

WE ARE HIS PEOPLE: the sheep of his flock.

PSALM REFRAIN - FOURTH SUNDAY OF EASTER - CYCLE C

Lord, let your mercy be on us, as we place our trust in you.

PSALM REFRAIN - FIFTH SUNDAY OF EASTER - CYCLE A

I will praise you, Lord, in the assembly of your people.

PSALM REFRAIN - FIFTH SUNDAY OF EASTER - CYCLE B

I will praise your name for ever, my king and my God.

PSALM REFRAIN - FIFTH SUNDAY OF EASTER - CYCLE C

Let all the earth cry out to God with joy.

PSALM REFRAIN - SIXTH SUNDAY OF EASTER - CYCLE A

THE LORD HAS REVEALED TO THE NATIONS HIS SAVING POWER.

PSALM REFRAIN - SIXTH SUNDAY OF EASTER - CYCLE B

O GOD, LET ALL THE NATIONS PRAISE YOU!

PSALM REFRAIN - SIXTH SUNDAY OF EASTER - CYCLE C

GOD MOUNTS HIS THRONE
TO SHOUTS OF JOY;
A BLARE OF TRUMPETS
FOR THE LORD.

PSALM REFRAIN - ASCENSION - CYCLES ABC

I believe that I shall see
the good things of the Lord
in the land of the living.

PSALM REFRAIN - SEVENTH SUNDAY OF EASTER - CYCLE A

The Lord has set his
throne in heaven.

PSALM REFRAIN - SEVENTH SUNDAY OF EASTER - CYCLE B

The Lord is king, the
most high over
all the earth.

PSALM REFRAIN - SEVENTH SUNDAY OF EASTER - CYCLE C

Lord, send out your Spirit, and renew the face of the earth.

PSALM REFRAIN - PENTECOST - VIGIL - CYCLES ABC

LORD, SEND OUT YOUR SPIRIT, AND RENEW THE FACE OF THE EARTH.

PSALM REFRAIN - PENTECOST SUNDAY - CYCLE ABC

HERE AM I, LORD; I COME TO DO YOUR WILL.

PSALM REFRAIN - SECOND SUNDAY OF THE YEAR - CYCLES AB

PROCLAIM HIS MARVELOUS DEEDS TO ALL THE NATIONS.

PSALM REFRAIN - SECOND SUNDAY OF THE YEAR - CYCLE C

The Lord is my light and my salvation.

PSALM REFRAIN - THIRD SUNDAY OF THE YEAR - CYCLE A

Teach me your ways, O Lord.

PSALM REFRAIN - THIRD SUNDAY OF THE YEAR - CYCLE B

Your words, Lord, are spirit and life.

PSALM REFRAIN - THIRD SUNDAY OF THE YEAR - CYCLE C

Happy the poor in spirit, the kingdom of heaven is theirs!

PSALM REFRAIN - FOURTH SUNDAY OF THE YEAR - CYCLE A

IF TODAY YOU HEAR HIS VOICE, HARDEN NOT YOUR HEARTS.

PSALM REFRAIN - FOURTH SUNDAY OF THE YEAR - CYCLE B

I WILL SING OF YOUR SALVATION.

PSALM REFRAIN - FOURTH SUNDAY OF THE YEAR - CYCLE C

THE JUST MAN IS A LIGHT IN DARKNESS TO THE UPRIGHT.

PSALM REFRAIN - FIFTH SUNDAY OF THE YEAR - CYCLE A

Praise the Lord who heals the brokenhearted.

PSALM REFRAIN - FIFTH SUNDAY OF THE YEAR - CYCLE B

In the sight of the angels I will sing your praises, Lord.

PSALM REFRAIN - FIFTH SUNDAY OF THE YEAR - CYCLE C

Happy are they who follow the law of the Lord!

PSALM REFRAIN - SIXTH SUNDAY OF THE YEAR - CYCLE A

I turn to you, Lord, in time of trouble, and you fill me with the joy of salvation.

PSALM REFRAIN - SIXTH SUNDAY OF THE YEAR - CYCLE B

HAPPY ARE THEY WHO HOPE IN THE LORD.

PSALM REFRAIN - SIXTH SUNDAY OF THE YEAR - CYCLE C

THE LORD IS KIND AND MERCIFUL.

PSALM REFRAIN - SEVENTH SUNDAY OF THE YEAR - CYCLE A

LORD, HEAL MY SOUL, FOR I HAVE SINNED AGAINST YOU.

PSALM REFRAIN - SEVENTH SUNDAY OF THE YEAR - CYCLE B

The Lord is kind and merciful.

PSALM REFRAIN - SEVENTH SUNDAY OF THE YEAR - CYCLE C

Rest in God alone, my soul.

PSALM REFRAIN - EIGHTH SUNDAY OF THE YEAR - CYCLE A

The Lord is kind and merciful.

PSALM REFRAIN - EIGHTH SUNDAY OF THE YEAR - CYCLE B

Lord, it is good to give thanks to you.

PSALM REFRAIN - EIGHTH SUNDAY OF THE YEAR - CYCLE C

LORD, BE MY ROCK OF SAFETY.

PSALM REFRAIN - NINTH SUNDAY OF THE YEAR - CYCLE A

SING WITH JOY TO GOD OUR HELP.

PSALM REFRAIN - NINTH SUNDAY OF THE YEAR - CYCLE B

GO OUT TO ALL THE WORLD, AND TELL THE GOOD NEWS.

PSALM REFRAIN - NINTH SUNDAY OF THE YEAR - CYCLE C

To the upright I will show the saving power of God.

PSALM REFRAIN - TENTH SUNDAY OF THE YEAR - CYCLE A

With the Lord there is mercy, and fullness of redemption.

PSALM REFRAIN - TENTH SUNDAY OF THE YEAR - CYCLE B

I will praise you, Lord, for you have rescued me.

PSALM REFRAIN - TENTH SUNDAY OF THE YEAR - CYCLE C

We are his people: the sheep of his flock.

PSALM REFRAIN - ELEVENTH SUNDAY OF THE YEAR - CYCLE A

LORD, IT IS GOOD TO GIVE THANKS TO YOU.

PSALM REFRAIN - ELEVENTH SUNDAY OF THE YEAR - CYCLE B

LORD, FORGIVE THE WRONG 1 HAVE DONE.

PSALM REFRAIN - ELEVENTH SUNDAY OF THE YEAR - CYCLE C

LORD, IN YOUR
GREAT LOVE,
ANSWER ME.

PSALM REFRAIN - TWELFTH SUNDAY OF THE YEAR - CYCLE A

Give thanks to the Lord,
his love is everlasting.

PSALM REFRAIN - TWELFTH SUNDAY OF THE YEAR - CYCLE B

My soul is thirsting for
you, O Lord my God.

PSALM REFRAIN - TWELFTH SUNDAY OF THE YEAR - CYCLE C

For ever I will sing the goodness of the Lord.

PSALM REFRAIN - THIRTEENTH SUNDAY OF THE YEAR - CYCLE A

I will praise you, Lord, for you have rescued me.

PSALM REFRAIN - THIRTEENTH SUNDAY OF THE YEAR - CYCLE B

YOU ARE MY INHERITANCE, O LORD.

PSALM REFRAIN - THIRTEENTH SUNDAY OF THE YEAR - CYCLE C

I WILL PRAISE YOUR NAME FOR EVER, MY KING AND MY GOD.

PSALM REFRAIN - FOURTEENTH SUNDAY OF THE YEAR - CYCLE A

OUR EYES ARE FIXED ON THE LORD, PLEADING FOR HIS MERCY.

PSALM REFRAIN - FOURTEENTH SUNDAY OF THE YEAR - CYCLE B

Let all the earth cry out to God with joy.

PSALM REFRAIN - FOURTEENTH SUNDAY OF THE YEAR - CYCLE C

The seed that falls on good ground will yield a fruitful harvest.

PSALM REFRAIN - FIFTEENTH SUNDAY OF THE YEAR - CYCLE A

Lord, let us see your kindness, and grant us your salvation.

PSALM REFRAIN - FIFTEENTH SUNDAY OF THE YEAR - CYCLE B

Turn to the Lord in your need, and you will live.

PSALM REFRAIN - FIFTEENTH SUNDAY OF THE YEAR - CYCLE C

LORD, YOU ARE GOOD AND FORGIVING.

THE LORD IS MY SHEPHERD; THERE IS NOTHING I SHALL WANT.

he who does justice will live in the presence of the Lord.

Lord, I love your commands.

PSALM REFRAIN - SEVENTEENTH SUNDAY OF THE YEAR - CYCLE A

The hand of the Lord feeds us, he answers all our needs.

PSALM REFRAIN - SEVENTEENTH SUNDAY OF THE YEAR - CYCLE B

Lord, on the day I called for help, you answered me.

PSALM REFRAIN - SEVENTEENTH SUNDAY OF THE YEAR - CYCLE C

The hand of the Lord feeds us; he answers all our needs.

PSALM REFRAIN - EIGHTEENTH SUNDAY OF THE YEAR - CYCLE A

THE LORD GAVE THEM BREAD FROM HEAVEN.

PSALM REFRAIN - EIGHTEENTH SUNDAY OF THE YEAR - CYCLE B

IF TODAY YOU HEAR HIS VOICE, HARDEN NOT YOUR HEARTS.

PSALM REFRAIN - EIGHTEENTH SUNDAY OF THE YEAR - CYCLE C

LORD, LET US SEE YOUR KINDNESS, AND GRANT US YOUR SALVATION.

PSALM REFRAIN - NINETEENTH SUNDAY OF THE YEAR - CYCLE A

Taste and see the goodness of the Lord.

PSALM REFRAIN - NINETEENTH SUNDAY OF THE YEAR - CYCLE B

Happy the people the Lord has chosen to be his own.

PSALM REFRAIN - NINETEENTH SUNDAY OF THE YEAR - CYCLE C

O God, let all the nations praise you!

PSALM REFRAIN - TWENTIETH SUNDAY OF THE YEAR - CYCLE A

Taste and see the goodness of the Lord.

PSALM REFRAIN - TWENTIETH SUNDAY OF THE YEAR - CYCLE B

LORD, COME TO MY AID!

PSALM REFRAIN - TWENTIETH SUNDAY OF THE YEAR - CYCLE C

LORD, YOUR LOVE IS ETERNAL; DO NOT FORSAKE THE WORK OF YOUR HANDS.

PSALM REFRAIN - TWENTY- FIRST SUNDAY OF THE YEAR - CYCLE A

TASTE AND SEE THE GOODNESS OF THE LORD.

PSALM REFRAIN - TWENTY- FIRST SUNDAY OF THE YEAR - CYCLE B

Go out to all the world and tell the Good News.

PSALM REFRAIN - TWENTY- FIRST SUNDAY OF THE YEAR - CYCLE C

My soul is thirsting for you, O Lord my God.

PSALM REFRAIN - TWENTY - SECOND SUNDAY OF THE YEAR - CYCLE A

He who does justice will live in the presence of the Lord.

PSALM REFRAIN - TWENTY - SECOND SUNDAY OF THE YEAR - CYCLE B

God, in your goodness, you have made a home for the poor.

PSALM REFRAIN - TWENTY - SECOND SUNDAY OF THE YEAR - CYCLE C

IF TODAY YOU HEAR HIS VOICE, HARDEN NOT YOUR HEARTS.

PSALM REFRAIN - TWENTY - THIRD SUNDAY OF THE YEAR - CYCLE A

PRAISE THE LORD MY SOUL !

PSALM REFRAIN - TWENTY - THIRD SUNDAY OF THE YEAR - CYCLE B

IN EVERY AGE, O LORD, YOU HAVE BEEN OUR REFUGE.

PSALM REFRAIN - TWENTY - THIRD SUNDAY OF THE YEAR - CYCLE C

The Lord is kind and merciful, slow to anger, and rich in compassion.

PSALM REFRAIN - TWENTY - FOURTH SUNDAY OF THE YEAR - CYCLE A

I will walk in the presence of the Lord, in the land of the living.

PSALM REFRAIN - TWENTY - FOURTH SUNDAY OF THE YEAR - CYCLE B

I will rise and go to my father.

PSALM REFRAIN - TWENTY - FOURTH SUNDAY OF THE YEAR - CYCLE C

The Lord is near to all who call him.

THE LORD UPHOLDS MY LIFE.

PRAISE THE LORD WHO LIFTS UP THE POOR.

REMEMBER YOUR MERCIES, O LORD.

PSALM REFRAIN - TWENTY - SIXTH SUNDAY OF THE YEAR - CYCLE A

The precepts of the Lord give joy to the heart.

PSALM REFRAIN - TWENTY - SIXTH SUNDAY OF THE YEAR - CYCLE B

Praise the Lord, my soul!

PSALM REFRAIN - TWENTY - SIXTH SUNDAY OF THE YEAR - CYCLE C

The vineyard of the Lord is the house of Israel.

PSALM REFRAIN - TWENTY - SEVENTH SUNDAY OF THE YEAR - CYCLE A

May the Lord bless us all the days of our lives.

PSALM REFRAIN - TWENTY - SEVENTH SUNDAY OF THE YEAR - CYCLE B

IF TODAY YOU HEAR HIS VOICE, HARDEN NOT YOUR HEARTS.

PSALM REFRAIN - TWENTY - SEVENTH SUNDAY OF THE YEAR - CYCLE C

I SHALL LIVE IN THE HOUSE OF THE LORD ALL THE DAYS OF MY LIFE.

PSALM REFRAIN - TWENTY - EIGHTH SUNDAY OF THE YEAR - CYCLE A

FILL US WITH YOUR LOVE, O LORD, AND WE WILL SING FOR JOY!

PSALM REFRAIN - TWENTY - EIGHTH SUNDAY OF THE YEAR - CYCLE B

The Lord has revealed to the nations his saving power.

PSALM REFRAIN - TWENTY - EIGHTH SUNDAY OF THE YEAR - CYCLE C

Give the Lord glory and honor.

PSALM REFRAIN - TWENTY - NINTH SUNDAY OF THE YEAR - CYCLE A

Lord, let your mercy be on us, as we place our trust in you.

PSALM REFRAIN - TWENTY - NINTH SUNDAY OF THE YEAR - CYCLE B

Our help is from the Lord who made heaven and earth.

PSALM REFRAIN - TWENTY - NINTH SUNDAY OF THE YEAR - CYCLE C

I LOVE YOU, LORD, MY STRENGTH.

PSALM REFRAIN - THIRTIETH SUNDAY OF THE YEAR - CYCLE A

THE LORD HAS DONE GREAT THINGS FOR US; WE ARE FILLED WITH JOY.

PSALM REFRAIN - THIRTIETH SUNDAY OF THE YEAR - CYCLE B

THE LORD HEARS THE CRY OF THE POOR.

PSALM REFRAIN - THIRTIETH SUNDAY OF THE YEAR - CYCLE C

In you, Lord, I have found my peace.

PSALM REFRAIN - THIRTY - FIRST SUNDAY OF THE YEAR - CYCLE A

I love you, Lord, my strength.

PSALM REFRAIN - THIRTY - FIRST SUNDAY OF THE YEAR - CYCLE B

I will praise your name for ever, my king and my God.

PSALM REFRAIN - THIRTY - FIRST SUNDAY OF THE YEAR - CYCLE C

My soul is thirsting for you, O Lord my God.

PSALM REFRAIN - THIRTY - SECOND SUNDAY OF THE YEAR - CYCLE A

PRAISE THE LORD, MY SOUL!

PSALM REFRAIN - THIRTY - SECOND SUNDAY OF THE YEAR - CYCLE B

LORD, WHEN YOUR GLORY APPEARS, MY JOY WILL BE FULL.

PSALM REFRAIN - THIRTY - SECOND SUNDAY OF THE YEAR - CYCLE C

HAPPY ARE THOSE WHO FEAR THE LORD.

PSALM REFRAIN - THIRTY - THIRD SUNDAY OF THE YEAR - CYCLE A

Keep me safe, O God: you are my hope.

PSALM REFRAIN - THIRTY - THIRD SUNDAY OF THE YEAR - CYCLE B

The Lord comes to rule the earth with justice.

PSALM REFRAIN - THIRTY - THIRD SUNDAY OF THE YEAR - CYCLE C

The Lord is my shepherd, there is nothing I shall want.

PSALM REFRAIN - THIRTY - FOURTH SUNDAY OF THE YEAR
CHRIST THE KING - CYCLE A

The Lord is king, he is robed in majesty.

PSALM REFRAIN - THIRTY - FOURTH SUNDAY OF THE YEAR
CHRIST THE KING - CYCLE B

I REJOICED WHEN I HEARD THEM SAY: LET US GO TO THE HOUSE OF THE LORD.

PSALM REFRAIN - THIRTY - FOURTH SUNDAY OF THE YEAR
CHRIST THE KING - CYCLE C

GLORY AND PRAISE
FOR EVER!

PSALM REFRAIN - SUNDAY AFTER PENTECOST - TRINITY SUNDAY - CYCLE A

happy the people
the Lord has chosen
to be his own.

PSALM REFRAIN - SUNDAY AFTER PENTECOST - TRINITY SUNDAY - CYCLE B

O Lord, our God, how wonderful
your name in all the earth.

PSALM REFRAIN - SUNDAY AFTER PENTECOST - TRINITY SUNDAY - CYCLE C

Praise the Lord, Jerusalem.

PSALM REFRAIN - THURSDAY AFTER TRINITY SUNDAY
CORPUS CHRISTI - CYCLE A

I will take the cup of salvation, and call on the name of the Lord.

PSALM REFRAIN - THURSDAY AFTER TRINITY SUNDAY
CORPUS CHRISTI - CYCLE B

You are a priest for ever, in the line of Melchizedek.

PSALM REFRAIN - THURSDAY AFTER TRINITY SUNDAY
CORPUS CHRISTI - CYCLE C

THE LORD'S KINDNESS IS EVERLASTING TO THOSE WHO FEAR HIM.

PSALM REFRAIN - FRIDAY OF THE SECOND WEEK AFTER PENTECOST
SACRED HEART - CYCLE A

YOU WILL DRAW WATER JOYFULLY FROM THE SPRINGS OF SALVATION.

PSALM REFRAIN - FRIDAY OF THE SECOND WEEK AFTER PENTECOST
SACRED HEART - CYCLE B

The LORD is my shepherd, THERE IS NOTHING I SHALL WANT.

PSALM REFRAIN - FRIDAY OF THE SECOND WEEK AFTER PENTECOST
SACRED HEART - CYCLE C